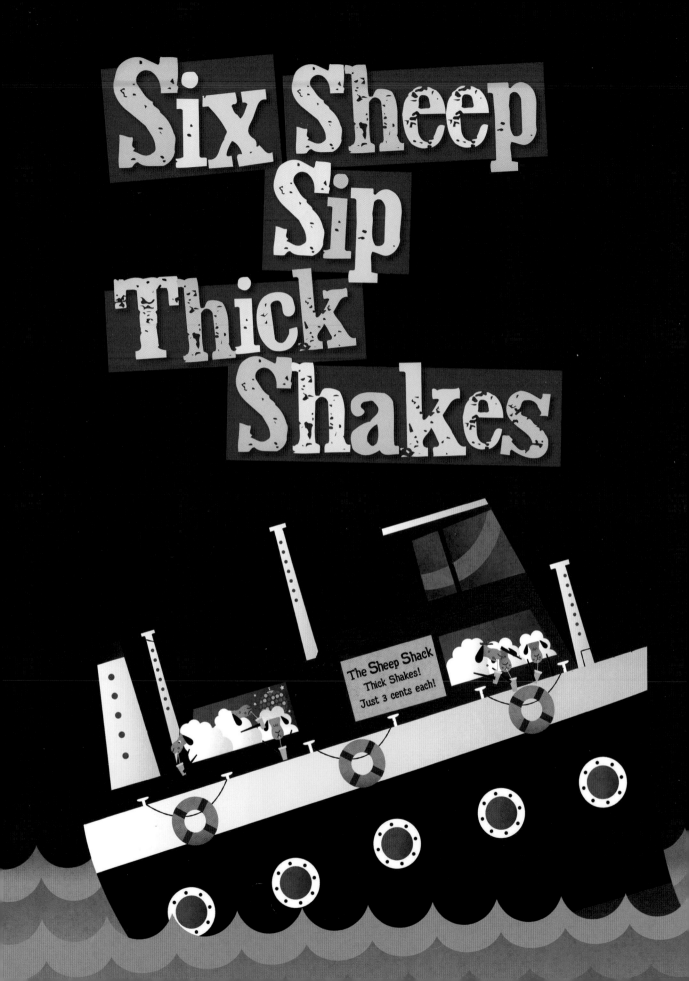

And Other Tricky

~~TWONGUE TISTERS~~

TONGUE TWISTERS

Brian P. Cleary

Illustrations by
Steve Mack

M
Millbrook Press ★ Minneapolis

Nan's knapsack straps sat on the striped steps.

The water in Flo's Inn flows in frozen.

The ghostly moans
were mostly groans.

See the Greek geeks
as they shoot
three free throws.

While the cat naps on the mat,
the gnats knit caps.

Miss Tish made a quick list of those she'd kissed quickest.

Sasha shifted as she sifted
through the thistle
for her sister's whistle.

Channel 1: All Movies, All the Time! ($5 per show)

Channel 2: Amazing Sports! ($10 per game)

Channel 3: Bunny News Network (fee free!!)

BUNNY NEWS NETWORK

3

BNN

The TV was fee-free for channel 3.

On Christmas Eve,
three thieves see
Steve's skis.

To: Steve

Sammy stammered as he told the stray in the sleigh to stay.

S-s-stay!

Mrs. Brack's brisket
in the black basket
is sold by the bunches
for breakfast
and brunches.

The people with the purple paper pranced in their pants by the simple steeple.

She sneezed
in her sleeve
as they seized
Mrs. Sleed.

Ahh-choo!

Few knew that Mr. Froo flew in the fleshy, freshly fried fish from Florida.

Brady and Blake broke blackened bread with Blake's brother, Blair.

Produce
Plaza

Plum Pudding
$10.00

PLUM PUDDING
PLUM PUDDING PLUM PUDDING
PLUM PUDDING PLUM PUDDING PLUM PUDDING
PLUM PUDDING PLUM PUDDING PLUM PUDDING PLUM PUDDI

Patty Packer placed a pint of pricey plum pudding on the platform at the produce plaza.

Fred frowned and fled frantically
when he found the
flounder in his bed.

Looking for ways to praise
Ray's plays, Ray's parents
applaud appropriately.

poot!

Tim and his thin twin sister, Trish, twice tricked their thick sitter.

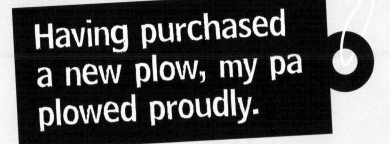

Having purchased a new plow, my pa plowed proudly.

She let the sheik sleep
on the sleek sheet.

As a favor,
my favorite flavor
was placed on my plate.

Six sick sheep on the steep ship
sip thick, cheap shakes
in the ship's chic
sheep shack.

Two-ton trains
transporting twelve three-toed turtles
twist trickily on the twin train tracks.

Make Your Own Tongue Twisters

You can make tongue twisters of your own! To find out how, first you'll need to learn how tongue twisters work—and just why they are so difficult to say out loud.

Tongue twisters are sentences or phrases that combine similar sounds in repetition. Often the more words there are in a tongue twister, the harder it is to pronounce each of the words the first time through. Sometimes, the similar sounds are at the beginning of the words, as in:

Sammy stammered as he told the stray in the sleigh to stay.

Note that the use of words beginning with s, st, str, and sl makes your tongue do all sorts of gymnastics to get the sentence right!

Other times, the "twist" is at the back end of the words, like it is here:

While the cat naps on the mat, the gnats knit caps.

The ending letters of t, ps, and ts are what cause all the commotion.

Certain letter combinations can be particularly difficult to pronounce. Take these, for example:

gr/gl/g
fr/fl/f
th/s/st/str
br/bl/b
pr/pl/p
sh/sl/s
sw/sl/st
tw/tr/t

The dictionary will give you bunches of words that start with these tongue-twister-friendly combinations. Take a look—and then get to work writing your own tongue twisters. Your own imagination is your only limitation!

To my friends at Price Laboratory School
—b.p.c.

For Alex and Ava, my two little art directors
—s.m.

Millbrook Press
A division of Lerner Publishing Group, Inc.
241 First Avenue North
Minneapolis, MN 55401 U.S.A.

Website address: www.lernerbooks.com

Library of Congress Cataloging-in-Publication Data

Cleary, Brian P., 1959–
    Six sheep sip thick shakes : and other tricky tongue twisters / by Brian P. Cleary ; illustrations by Steve Mack.
        p.   cm.
    ISBN: 978–1–58013–585–6 (lib. bdg. : alk. paper)
    1. Tongue twisters. I. Mack, Steve (Steve Page), ill.
    II. Title.
    PN6371.5.C54 2011
    398.8—dc22   2010014421

Manufactured in the United States of America
1 - CG - 12/15/10